D0461727

Women Who Rock

WITHDRAWN

DEMI Lovato

GAIL TERP

WORLD BOOK

BOLT

This World Book edition of *Demi Lovato*
is published by agreement between
Black Rabbit Books and World Book, Inc.
© 2017 Black Rabbit Books,
2140 Howard Dr. West,
North Mankato, MN 56003 U.S.A.
World Book, Inc.,
180 North LaSalle St., Suite 900,
Chicago, IL 60601 U.S.A.

Design and Production by Michael Sellner
Photo Research by Rhonda Milbrett

Library of Congress Control Number: 2015954914

HC ISBN: 978-0-7166-9449-6   PB ISBN: 978-0-7166-9450-2

Printed in the United States at CG Book Printers,
North Mankato, Minnesota, 56003. PO #1799 4/16

Contents

CHAPTER 1

A Strong Singer

The words to her song "Skyscraper" tell a lot. "Go on and try to tear me down. I will be rising from the ground. Like a skyscraper." When Demi Lovato sings those words, she is fierce. She shows her power. And her fans love it.

Superstar

The words to "Skyscraper" remind Lovato to be strong. Her life has been hard. She did drugs. She hurt herself. But then she got help. This song reminds her she'll be OK.

Lovato is a superstar. She's a musician with millions of fans. She's an actress and an author too. And she uses her **fame** to help others.

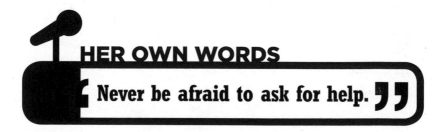

HER OWN WORDS

Never be afraid to ask for help. **" "**

Fun Facts

WAS A JUDGE
ON THE TV SHOW
THE X FACTOR

FULL NAME IS
DEMETRIA DEVONNE LOVATO

6'

5'

4'

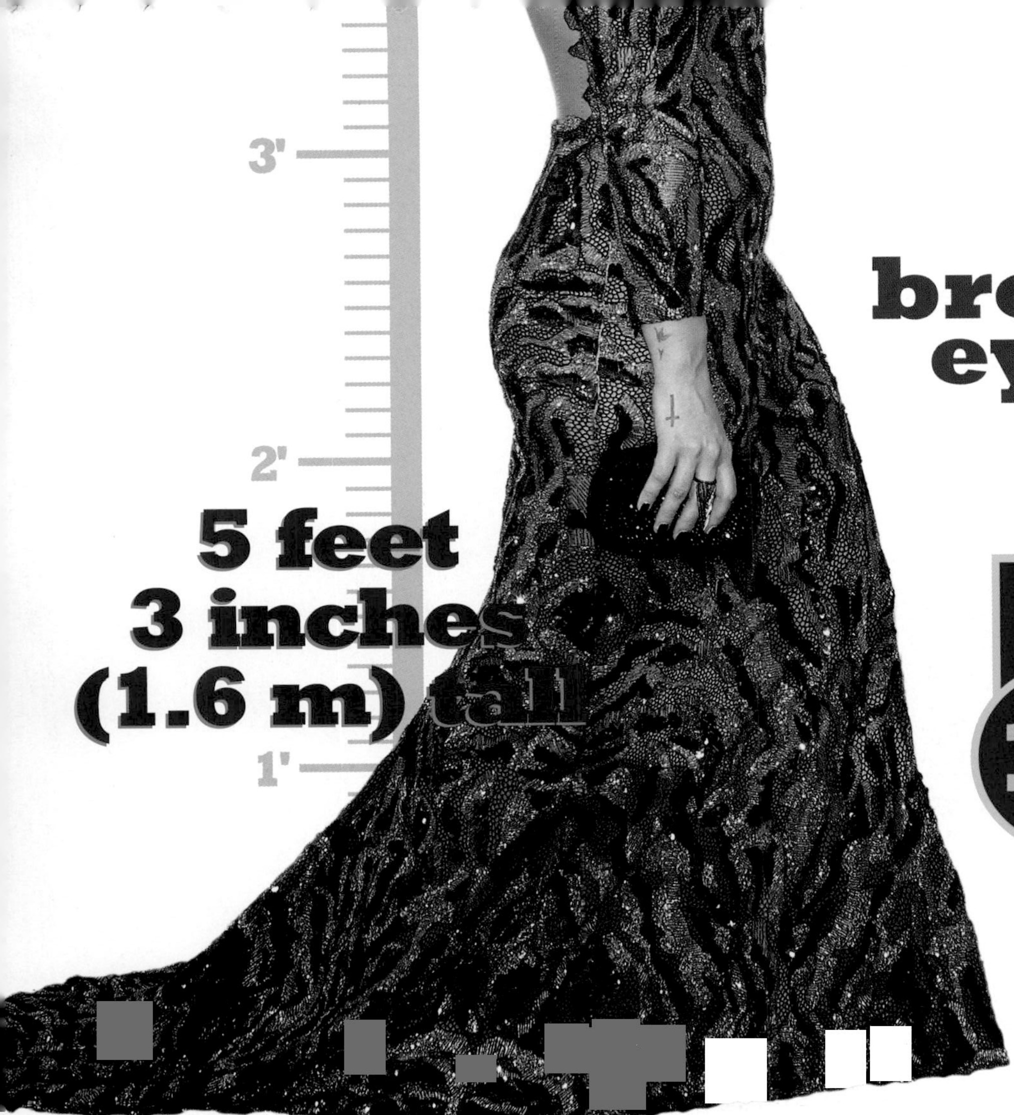

brown eyes

BOUGHT HER FAMILY A HOUSE ON HER **18**TH BIRTHDAY

IS ALLERGIC TO CATS

5 feet 3 inches (1.6 m) tall

3'
2'
1'

CHAPTER 2

Years

Lovato was born August 20, 1992. As a kid, she loved to sing. She loved to act too. When she was 10, she got a part on the show *Barney & Friends*. Lovato stayed with the show for two years.

Being Bullied

Lovato was clearly talented. But when she was 12, kids at school **bullied** her. Her parents took her out of school. They **homeschooled** her. At age 15, Lovato and her family moved to Hollywood. They thought it was the best place for a girl with talent.

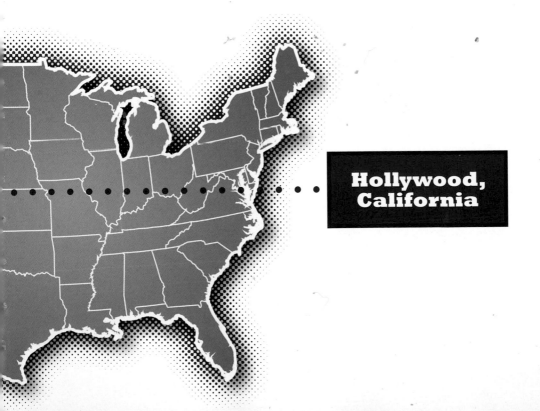

Hollywood, California

Busy Lovato

The years 2008 and 2009 were crazy for Lovato. She did a lot. And her fame grew.

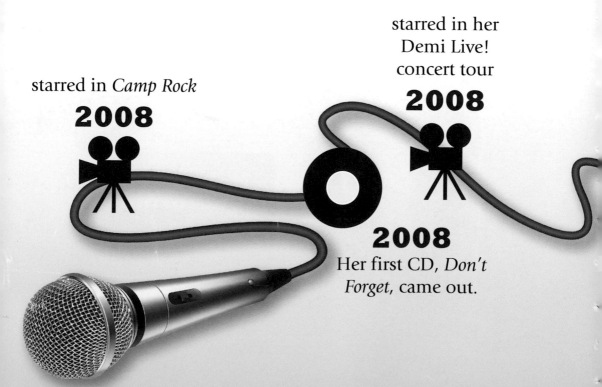

starred in *Camp Rock*
2008

starred in her Demi Live! concert tour
2008

2008
Her first CD, *Don't Forget*, came out.

2009
starred in *Sonny with a Chance* TV show

2009
starred in
*Princess Protection
Program* movie

2009
Her
Here We Go Again
CD came out.

CHAPTER 3

Making It

Soon after moving, Lovato got parts on the Disney Channel. In 2008, she **starred** in the movie *Camp Rock*. She played a young singer. This **role** helped make her famous.

Lovato worked with Nick Jonas on *CAMP ROCK*. The two are still best friends.

FAMOUS
FRIENDS

Selena Gomez and Lovato met working on *BARNEY & FRIENDS.*

Lovato and Miley Cyrus' friendship started on the Disney channel. But they're not friends anymore.

Staying Strong

Being so busy was too much for Lovato. She used drugs. She started hurting herself. In 2010, Lovato went to a **treatment center**. While there, she learned how to take care of herself. She no longer uses drugs. She exercises each day.

After treatment, Lovato made a video called "Stay Strong." She spoke of her struggles. She wanted to help others who have problems.

New Music

Lovato went on to make more great music. *Unbroken* came out in 2011. The song "Skyscraper" was on this album. *Demi* came out in 2013. Both albums did very well. Each had more than $1 million in sales.

Lovato's Top 5 Billboard Hits (through 2015)

HIGHEST POSITION HOT 100 CHARTS

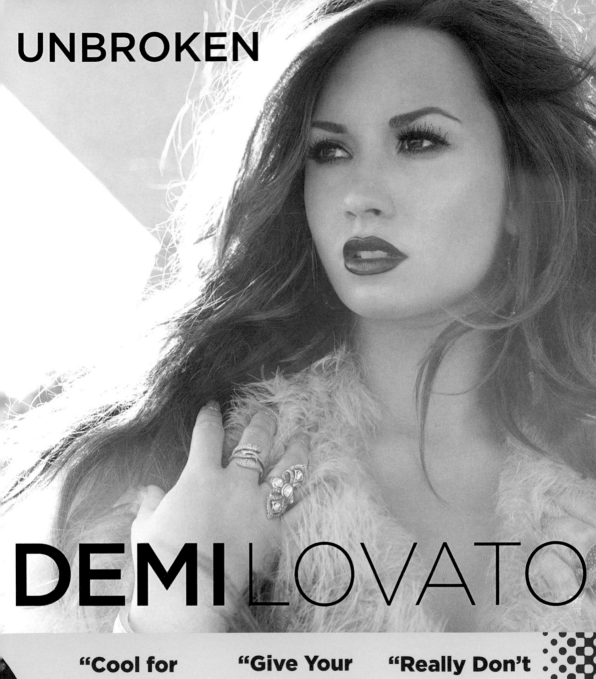

UNBROKEN

DEMI LOVATO

"Cool for the Summer"	"Give Your Heart a Break"	"Really Don't Care!"
11	16	26

"Heart Attack"	"Neon Lights"
10	36

CHAPTER 4

Lovato Today

In 2014, Lovato recorded "Let It Go." This song was in the movie *Frozen*. The movie was a huge hit. Lovato's song sold more than 1 million copies.

In 2015, Lovato's fifth album came out. *Confident* shows how Lovato has grown stronger. She's more confident in her life and in her music.

Lovato's fans are called "Lovatics."

MEAN STINKS PROGRAM

works to stop bullying

THE LOVATO TREATMENT SCHOLARSHIP PROGRAM

started and helps pay for a program for people with mental illnesses

FREE THE CHILDREN

raised more than $50,000 to build schools in poor countries

STOMP OUT BULLYING

raises money to stop bullying

TEENS FOR JEANS

asks kids to donate jeans

In the Spotlight

Lovato's future looks bright. She shows others how to be strong and successful. No one can doubt she has star power. She's likely to be in the spotlight for years to come.

Lovato started her own music label. She owns it with two friends. The label is called Safehouse Records.

TIMELINE

acted on *Barney & Friends*

2002–2004

2006

2008

1992 born in New Mexico

2005

2007

released *Don't Forget*

starred in *Camp Rock*

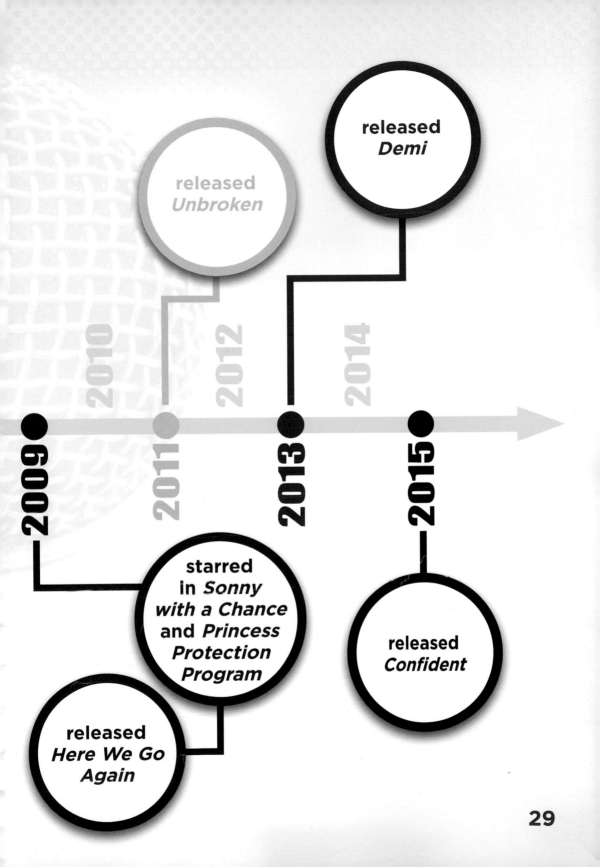

released
Demi

released
Unbroken

2010

2012

2014

2009

2011

2013

2015

starred
in *Sonny
with a Chance*
and *Princess
Protection
Program*

released
Confident

released
*Here We Go
Again*

allergic (uh-LUR-jik)—having a medical condition that causes someone to become sick after eating, touching, or breathing something that is harmless to most people

bully (BUL-ee)—to fighten, hurt, or threaten someone

fame (FAYM)—being known or recognized by many people

homeschool (HOM-skool)—to teach children at home instead of sending them to school

mental illness (MEN-tuhl IL-nuhs)— a problem that affects the mind and emotions

role (ROHL)—the character played by an actor

star (STAR)—to play the most important part in a movie, play, or TV show.

treatment center (TREET-muhnt SEN-tur)—a place that offers help to people with drug and alcohol problems

BOOKS

Peppas, Lynn. *Demi Lovato. Superstars!* New York: Crabtree Publishing Company, 2013.

Rajczak, Kristen. *Demi Lovato. Rising Stars.* New York: Gareth Stevens Pub., 2012.

Shaffer, Jody Jensen. *Demi Lovato: Taking Another Chance. Pop Culture Bios: Superstars.* Minneapolis: Lerner Publications Company, 2014.

WEBSITES

Demi Lovato Fun Facts
www.kidzworld.com/article/ 27024-demi-lovato-fun-facts

Stop Bullying.gov
www.stopbullying.gov/kids

INDEX